T0195694

Sweet Adeline

A Mother's Kitchen Poetry
and
Her Son's Retrospections

Sweet Adeline

A Mother's Kitchen Poetry
and
Her Son's Retrospections

ROBERT L. BRUNKER

WESTBOW
PRESS®
A DIVISION OF THOMAS NELSON
& ZONDERVAN

WestBow Press books may be ordered through
booksellers or by contacting:

WestBow Press
A Division of Thomas Nelson & Zondervan
1663 Liberty Drive
Bloomington, IN 47403
www.westbowpress.com
844-714-3454

Scripture taken from the King James Version of the Bible.

ISBN: 978-1-6642-7680-2 (sc)
ISBN: 978-1-6642-7679-6 (e)

Print information available on the last page.

WestBow Press rev. date: 11/17/2022

Contents

Preface   vii

Chapter 1	The Escape	1
Chapter 2	Another Mother and Another	11
Chapter 3	The Lean Years	24
Chapter 4	The Silence of the Empty Nest	40
Chapter 5	Alzheimer's, the Last Assault of Satan	61

Acknowledgments   75

About the Author   77

Preface

Paul Simon's moving lyrics to the "Dangling Conversation" contains the words "you read your Emily Dickenson and I my Robert Frost and we use bookmarks to measure what we lost." My mother's "Kitchen Poetry" does not have the degree of creativity of Dickenson, Frost or Simon. But these gifted people do not surpass the intensity of emotion nor sincerity of my simple mother's rhyming of her middle-class values of God, love of family, marriage, and friendship. Adeline is more likely not "to measure what she lost" but what she *gained* by God's grace. God is her bookmark and unabashed love is her meter.

The structure of her poetry is absent of syncopated rhyme of Simon and absent of the cadence of Phil Silverstein's "Giving Tree." Her poetry, written on the kitchen table during her empty nest years, filled her creative needs while fixing meals and canning vegetables for her husband. Her work is straight meter rhyme with a voice of recognition of God's overwhelming Grace. She was a woman given a litany of sorrows but refused to let Satan drown her in sorrow. She recognized beauty all around her and even the evil of Alzheimer's could not break her.

Adeline writes about what is around her and on a face value level uniquely seen through the lens of belief in God. So expect not fancy twists of meaning or precision of syncopated rhyme but like one who wraps the blanket of belief around her and writes of her dreams. Do expect middle class Christian morality to blossom out of a WYSIWYG (what you see is what you get) woman that trusts her savior to provide what she needs and to provide, through her, things that her contacts need. She lived up to the expectations of being a good shepherd that even Lynn Anderson (author of _They Smell Like Sheep_) would admire.

Her poetry was written for herself and her closest friends. By themselves and without explanation of the background of the author and without inside information on it's meaning, the poetry would probably be unworthy of publication—the worthiness comes through her life supporting her poetry. The revealed richness is too great to allow a select few to enjoy it. I believe that God placed this woman in her community for a purpose. Satan could not bring her down. Regardless of all her hardships she remained a believer, faced life with joy, and loved her husband with all her heart. Just maybe a part of that purpose was for her son to pull the flax seeds from this Holy linen. I am sure the weakness of this effort will be my interpretation and attempts to reveal the fullness of her works. May God grant the Grace of his intention so you will see His will through the words of Sweet Adeline— that is my prayer for this book.

Chapter One

THE ESCAPE

"I am going to have to get these kids to Knob Noster," thought Floyd as he studied the train schedules. "They are not going to let me take their grandchildren. My only chance to get these kids out of Boston is to sneak away in the middle of the night. Mom and Annabel will take care of them for me. I will go wherever to get a job; I can drive a truck for anybody."

Floyd planned his escape route. The maternal grandparents were rumored to be an important part of the Boston mafia and Floyd did not want to find out if that community belief were true. Floyd and Adelina Marta were married just eleven months before they had a son, Tom. Then after that a daughter in another two years. The mother died at her birth from hemorrhaging and in his wife's honor named the child after her, Adeline Martha Skillman.

Adeline's grandpa was a first-generation Italian immigrant and owned an important company in Boston.

They imported olive oil, citric fruits, bananas, and other produce and delivered to the grocery stores in the area. The business was doing well, and the family was well off.

Floyd got to know Adelina as he was a truck driver that had a back-and-forth route to Kansas City. She worked at her father's business in the office where the shipping papers were processed. Since being released from the marines in Boston after a two-year hitch, mainly driving trucks and doing guard duty, he got a job in Boston doing what he knew best—driving a truck. He traveled back and forth like a machine from his home base in Boston to Kansas City and back to Boston. Often he would have a load of olive oil and bananas and citrus. The produce had to be delivered in a timely way and trains did not work well for the produce.

Floyd, two-year old Tom, and two-week old Adeline huddled in the train station out of the way of plain site. A man with a newborn and toddler stands out and Floyd did not want to stand out. The interconnections of his father-in-law were sizable and not fully known by Floyd. His suitcase was stashed with supplies for the children. Another shirt and a change of underwear was the only thing packed for himself. Would he have enough money and enough supplies to get a newborn to Sedalia? He was going to depend on the diner car for some help and a lot of help from God.

Floyd was a soft spoken, sincere sounding man that people responded to well. As the trip ground on, the people in the seats around him were told the condensed version of the truth. He told them his wife died giving birth to Adeline and he was trying to get back to his family in Missouri to help him with the kids.

God was with Floyd. A passenger two rows up also was traveling with an older infant that was still nursing. After Floyd's too little supplies for Adeline was expended, the mother volunteered to nurse Adeline. Nursing was quite common in those days, even for an extended time. Other women on the train extended their kindness; they would take turns holding the baby to give Floyd's arms a rest. Women are drawn to an infant and want to hold them. Floyd was able to stretch his aching arms and legs. He was able to take care of Tom on those relief cycles.

Tom, despite his youthful age, somehow had discerned a sense of emergency and behaved as perfectly as one could expect. The trip although very tiring for all, went well and a sense of relief was shared by Floyd and Tom as they pulled into the Sedalia station to a reception of grandma and aunt Nana.

What would happen to the Boston trio? Could Floyd find work? What family members would come forward and help in these challenging economic times? Would Boston connections network to a small country town with a name like Knob Noster? Tensions created by these questions dissipated over time after watching any new people in town come and go. The trio was safe in the bosom of Knob Noster.

We are cautioned by our Lord not to judge other people. The old saying goes "don't judge a man unless you have walked a mile in his shoes" has truth. Floyd's shoes took him down some rough roads. In his lifetime, he lost a wife in childbirth, lost two children at birth (one in a second marriage years later), served at the end of World War I as a Marine, and as an enlisted Army soldier later in World War II. How much action did he see? He would not talk about it. He learned to roll his own cigarettes in WWII. As a kid, I saved the cloth bags for my marbles. He taught me how to play marbles and gave me my first batch.

I cannot say he was an ambitious man, but he would work on projects that would interest him between jobs, but the projects were always of limited duration. He did not miss work when he was employed. But he kept changing jobs, the depression saw to that. I think he would have been happier if he drove a taxi. He always enjoyed talking with people and never seemed to be anxious about just sitting and waiting on people when he drove people to a destination or delivered goods. I never knew him to be involved in a traffic accident.

He was slim and seemed to be bothered by allergies and "asthma." He would use an old over the counter remedy sold in cans that you burned and inhaled the smoke. It stunk, but maybe God used that because I never was tempted to try marihuana in college. The two "weeds" had a similar smell and I disliked them both. My dad was a strong, hardworking man and never smoked. The contrast of dad and grandad I am thankful for to this day.

One unusual remembrance of Floyd is that he always had clean clothes and his shirt was always pressed. If it were not pressed, he was ill. His characteristic dress was a striped blue and gray pair of overalls with a blue or gray solid colored work shirt—nicely ironed. I have no memory of him in any other ensemble.

Floyd would come and go in our family setting until his death. He always seemed to come when there was ample room for him. Our family moved several times in my first 20 years and Dad always had a job, but opportunities moved us several times in a relatively small area in Northwest Missouri. In those several homes my family occupied, there were extra rooms or extra buildings that Floyd could homestead in, not too far from the dinner table.

Floyd, for a period of years, took care of his two elderly uncles that lived together on an old run-down farm they had been living on for decades. Floyd was younger and could take care of the farm chores and garden and could drive the brothers to town for supplies and to see the doctors.

They lived in an old farmhouse with electricity but no inside running water. The house was heated by coal, the cookstove was corn cob fired and the kitchen had an aroma from hundreds of meals of butchered beef and pork produced on the farm. Vegetables came from the garden fresh or were canned in a diverse collection of jars that were clear, green, or blue tinted. About the only things they bought from the grocery store were flour, sugar, coffee, salt, and canning supplies. In the last few years they added bread, milk, and butter. I learned how to churn butter from Uncles "Bush" and "Tom."

My uncle Tom's (Sweet Adeline's brother) name came from both the old bachelor and from his grandfather. Bush and Tom were one source of Adeline's self-esteem, for they were always gentlemen and treated her like a little queen. I learned a few life lessons on visits there without realization until a couple of scores of years later.

My life has been a unique collection of life experiences. My formative years overlapped the generation tempered by the Great Depression tolerating demanding work, shortages, and a world war and the next generation that flourished in post war development. I am a "country" baby boomer—I am appreciative of the country aspect. I assimilated the middle-class values of hard work, marriage, family, generosity, and morality. As I finish writing these words after some laid fallow for twenty-six years and now, during the post-pandemic chaos of the 2020's, I hope I have transferred those values to my children that are raising the new generation.

The Little Red School House

The little red schoolhouse on top of the hill
Every time I go by it gives me a thrill.
It may have a crack in a window or two,
But I remember when it was brand new.

Many old memories come back to mind
From that little red schoolhouse I left behind.
I remember Jonnie, Bill, Mary, Jane, and May
And all the many good times we had at play.

The water from the well was as cold as could be
In the corner of the yard was the old oak tree.
From two big limbs hung our two rope swings.
We would swing away and how we girls would
　　sing.

By the side of school the boys played ball.
The girls were not allowed to play at all.
Sometime we girls would beg ourselves in
To the boys surprise the girls could win.

We loved our teacher and thought she was great,
She never scolded us when we were late.
We all saved our pennies for quite awhile
To buy her a Christmas gift; she would always smile.

We all walked home on the old dusty road.
The boys always seemed to find a fat toad.
They would chase us girls most every day.
I think we all liked it a little anyway.

We each have gone our many different ways.
I shall never forget those childhood days.
In my life they shall always be a precious part.
The little red schoolhouse is deep in my heart.

Sweet Adeline's primary grades were at a one room schoolhouse before consolidation of the little districts of the county. The tiny schools were coalesced into larger districts and school buses were run on "all weather" pavement or gravel roads. During wet weather the kids on dirt roads had to walk to a pickup point. In snowy weather of fairly rare times, farm tractors driven by one of the parents would pick up their kids. They would hang on tight for the short ride home. In all the stories covering those times, I never learned of any child falling off and getting hurt or run over. Kids were more aware, and parents were more attentive. There were no cell phones to distract them. In fact most of the homes did not have phones. But one thing the kids did do in those days—they wore their coats to and from school. Walking a quarter or half mile was common. They knew that they would have to endure whatever weather came. There were no plush vinyl seats and air-conditioned cars in those days. The buses were always cold in the winter.

That school was never red. It was always white, and it is to this day! Years later my parents bought and ran an old-time general store one mile from that schoolhouse. Starting around twelve years of age I would help put up hay for the farmer that bought that old schoolhouse. They put up a lean-to hay shed all around that schoolhouse and it stands and is used for that purpose today. That 100-year-old schoolhouse has been preserved by the metal shed built around it. I did not go to formal school there, but I learned several lessons in that shed housing the "school of hard knocks."

Although the school bus was cold in the winter, it did pick me up and drop me off in front of our house. But I always wore a coat in season, and I never left it at school!

I will let my unabashed prejudice ring forth. Those old one room schoolhouses were supported by the community and taught many times by an older dedicated woman of the community or a recent sharp graduate that took a short-term course for preparation of teaching. The no-nonsense curriculum essentially was reading, writing, arithmetic, and history. Void was sex education (they got that on the farm) and criticism of the government. The history they got was positive and generated pride in the freedom we enjoy. The local church, many times in the same plot of land as the schoolyard, was attended by the same children that went there to church and was an extension of the school. In both places they learned that the morals of Christianity were to be used in secular life, called citizenship. The term "woke" was referred to as a verb meaning to "wake up" from sleep. There was little bullying. The children learned to print, as well as, to write in "longhand." Arithmetic was on base 10, except for telling time and all students memorized their multiplication tables.

Find an old copy of depression era eighth grade graduation tests and see if you can pass it. You will be surprised by the complexity of it. If your grandchildren are in high school or beyond challenge them to take it. Be braced for disappointment.

Yes, there can be a few educational arguments on eliminating cursive writing, eliminating memorization of multiplication tables, and working in more than base 10, but other educators could give you sound opposing arguments. My point, now that I got that venom out of my system, is primary education needs to go back to the basics and have true basic education devoid of manipulative agendas by party politics. Our schools are failing in many ways; most citizens know it; most citizens know the primary trouble spots; and most citizens even know how to greatly improve them. The problem is the government is not the source of the solution. The problem is simplistic, but it has supernatural opposition; the solution is Christian revival. And we will continue to struggle until a divine intervention. It's a simple answer that is extremely unpopular

Sweet Adeline lived a life of many adjustments to maneuver around happenings that could have stimulated her to take a different pathway. She never felt sorry for herself. The intentional life lesson that she taught me directly, and announced that intention as she taught it to me, was a quote. The source remains unknown to me. Her life lesson: "I felt sorry for myself because I had no shoes, until I met a man with no feet." Some literally hate that classic proverb because the man with no shoes still had a problem, but Mom consistently decided to look on the brighter side of life.

She learned to look upon life as "a beautiful place to be." She learned that we live in a cursed creation after the fall of man and warns "just be thankful in this world to be born, but remember no perfect rose is without a thorn." Consider this wisdom in her poem, "Life."

Life

Life can be a beautiful place to be
Just behold all the beautiful things to see.
Look upon fields where wildflowers grow
And the mountain top covered with snow.

Seeing floating clouds in a bright blue sky above,
Listening to the soft cooing of a snow-white dove,
Seeing the red cardinal and the bright blue jay,
All brighten up our wintery days.

A walk after a rain on a warm spring day,
Watching little children in the puddles as they play,
Seeing across the sky a forming colorful rainbow,
Suddenly our hearts become all aglow.

All nature's beauty is from God above,
To us from His abounding love.
Just be thankful in this world to be born,
But remember no perfect rose is without a thorn.

Chapter Two

ANOTHER MOTHER
AND ANOTHER

After the Boston trio arrived in Knob Noster, they lived with Floyd's parents, Mattie and Thomas Skillman. Thomas owned a local general store and haberdashery. Floyd worked with his father, for only a brief time and worked on the neighboring farm of Uncles Tom and Bush, Mattie's brothers. Floyd was surrounded by three Tom's— son, father, and uncle. I doubt it was the abundance of Tom's that drove Floyd away. Soon Floyd was off to St. Louis to find work and after that he was generally a father in abstentia.

Sweet Adeline and her brother Tom were "parented" mainly by Mattie, whom they called "Mama." The foster father Thomas Skillman died a few years later—another loss in a series for Sweet Adeline. This loss was compounded by the loss of the home that burned to the ground during the Great Depression. Now what was to happen to Sweet

Adeline, brother Tom and grandma Mattie? She overheard the family in the next room talking; she quietly listened for the revelation of her fate. Government, especially in the depression days stayed out of family business when families divided up the children following tragedies.

"I will take Adeline," declared Annabel in a way that was final and not to be challenged. She had taken a course after graduating from high school, given to prepare teachers in those days. Annabel had been teaching school for a few years, had a husband, and a baby on the way.

"We will take Tom," Carl and Maxine agreed. Carl was a married younger brother of Floyd. Annabel and her husband, Robert, and eventually my namesake when I popped up years later, had bought a farm in Northwest Missouri. Carl and Maxine kept Mattie and Tom on the farm and Sweet Adeline went to live with her aunt Annabel and uncle Bob in Maryville—sixty miles away.

Floyd was single, getting work wherever he could, and was basically left out of the decision process. A woman in the home would be needed if Annabel had any say in the division and Floyd did not have a woman.

So now, Annabel would be the third mother of Sweet Adeline—a strict Godsend.

Annabel Hubble was a work of genteel art that, I'm sad to say, no longer exists. (I am writing this "retrospection" in my mid-fifties and will set it aside for another score of years! Many of the retrospections were written in my fifties and sixties and then revised. I ignore some of the redundancy. This is a "bucket list" project.) She was comfortable in overalls or lace and was equally dignified in both. She could pluck a chicken, milk a cow, quote Shakespeare, tutor a slow child, teach an adult Sunday school lesson, wipe a tear, and prepare a family reunion meal while leading the main conversation—and never once look at any cookbook. She unknowingly set the stage for women's liberation, but she would be disgusted today at the movement's diluted values and morality. She promoted high self-esteem in all the family's young and positively affected our value system by living the very values she taught. Cross her and you would have your hands full. I miss her terribly.

The indelible image I have of her dates back to the mid-nineteen fifties when she drove an Oldsmobile and always arrived wearing a black hat with a wide full brim, black purse, black shoes, and a flowing dress of taste but always modest price. Her hair was braided and wrapped tightly around her head like a crown. When she unwrapped it to comb it out it would just touch the floor. I think I was in my teens when she finally cut it short. I am sure she was more comfortable, but I was not. I will always remember my "Aunt Nana" very fondly that way— an image I cherish.

An image of her that I do not cherish, but is unfortunately as indelible, is one when I was asked to see her in the nursing home to check her teeth when her daughter thought she might be in pain. That was the first time she did not recognize me—my pain was unbearable. Even a few years earlier when she had a mild stroke and had a recent memory loss she immediately smiled upon my entering the room and called me by name. The doctor followed me into the room and during the exam asked her who the President of the United States was. She thought for a moment. This woman was always ready to talk politics and could list all the state and national main officers, but suddenly she realized she did not know. Too proud to ignore the question, she simply said she did not know.

After the departure of the physician, she asked her son-in-law in the room, "Who is the President of the United States?"

"Ronald Reagan," her son-in-law replied.

"Who? The actor?" When she got a positive nod she was astonished! She asked several times over if that were true. She regained all her memory after that, but that was a shock for a Truman Democrat to find that out!

She knew who I was, even though she did not know who the President of the United States was. She knew who I was. But when I went to that nursing home filled with an aroma of urine and disinfectant, she looked at me with a fixed focus. I know she was scanning her memory banks for the memory of a familiar face, but she did not retrieve the file. I was gone. Now she is gone. And so too are the opportunities to stop by to see her on my way home from my office. I did so occasionally. Not nearly enough times, I regret.

Sweet Adeline endured another separation. She had a deceased mother, a father in abstentia, a passed grandmother that was raising her that she called "Mama," and now she would be separated from her brother. The distance between the homes was sixty miles, so visits would be infrequent due to the great depression days.

My mother used her poetry to express a wide range of thoughts. The second poem presented here is not typical in that it did not exude happiness like the others. She was creative and looked at the bigger picture. Connections to her poetry was not always direct; she surprisingly used symbolisms so strict that you were unaware of them being used. In discussing this poem and a later poem entitled "A Young Soldier" with my sister, her comments were: "Sometimes it was a bit hard to understand where her ideas were coming from, but she knew what she wanted to say." Creative people will many times carry an emotional tug to other emotions or personify them in another way to express them. She intuitively used this poetic license. I became aware of this when Adeline informed me that her poem "A Young Soldier", mentioned above, was stimulated by a drawing of a bird given to her by her son-in-law. Consider this next poem. What symbolisms were being used?

Happiness

Clouds pass over me, gray is the day.
Only loneliness is a companion to me.
Happiness, oh happiness, where do you stay?
I have searched so long, where could you be?

The days come and make the weeks.
The months come and go into years.
Oh for happiness, I do earnestly seek.
My eyes now growing dim with tears.

The beauty of music is no longer.
I am engulfed with loneliness.
The fear of each day is growing stronger
You are a stranger to me, dear happiness.

Despair and anguish tear at my heart.
All I cherished and loved is gone.
Joy and laughter I have no part.
All night through I dread the dawn.

If this is the path I must trod,
Wanting and looking for things that can't be,
If so, may I soon be covered with sod.
May after death then be a happier place for me.

In so many ways my mother declared her happiness –in her poetry, her actions, and in her everyday words. Her poem "Happiness" seems out of character; perhaps a better title more consistent with her everyday demeaner would he "Loneliness." She is equating being unhappy with being lonely. It would be extremely hard for a woman that was such a "hands on" mother, in a people-oriented retail business, and so active in her church activities to be resigned to be the domestic engineer of an empty nest. She was not a woman seeking to enjoy peace and quiet except in her walks in nature.

My parents attended essentially all school athletic events, all school functions that any of the children were involved, and all church events. Rarely were community major events missed. To be so active and focused on the activities of your children only to have them, over a course of a few years, move out of the house and be left alone with no activities in which to be involved was shocking to them. The continually active involvement of their children was their social life. To them it was not going to a boring little league baseball game and sitting on hard bleachers; it was going to an event where all your friends were attending, where the sense of community dwelled, and where their entertainment was found.

Even though my mother for many years worked in the family business where the adjacent home housed their children at all times, she was essentially a full-time mother and full-time clerk, from seven in the morning till nine at night for six or even seven days a week. To have all your children leave the nest in your prime would be like forced retirement on a career woman who loved her job. I was the first to leave for college and she was just thirty-eight!

Take away the profession from a man and many will say they would rather die than be idle and of no value to society. We treat our elderly like our finest china, we put them away in storage out of the way of the busyness of everyday activities and bring them out of storage on special occasions.

The" unhappiness" she was experiencing was the taunt of loneliness. She declares in her poem "All I cherished and loved is gone." She says, "The beauty of music is no longer. I am engulfed with loneliness." The "music" is the sounds of the family, and no one is there to generate the notes of that family melody. The next verse she says, "Joy and laughter I have no part."

Most of the elderly suffer from separation sickness from our God and mothers compound that ache in their heart with the yearning for their children. All while being constantly reminded of their loneliness by pictures and mementos lining their empty nest. Happiness is not the "stranger" she declares—it is her children too busy in their own families and careers. She was prophetic in her lines "the fear of each day is growing stronger." Her Alzheimer's later created unhappiness and fears without cause and without warning. Soon her empty nest, despite the engulfing loneliness will become the only haven from her increasing nocturnal fears.

The cruelty of parenthood is the all too brief time of our joy in being the center of attention of our children in their early lives. The joy of parenthood quickly evolves into the remembrance of times past—a mental movie that is available at our whim. She says, "the beauty of music is no longer." Her silent home without the music of her children's everyday activities is her source of loneliness. Replaying her mental movies are no longer enough. Each playing places another scratch on the image and the colors begin to fade, the crispness of the facial images blur, and the brilliance dims. Unhappiness for Adeline was being forced to live in the past.

In addition, consider that essentially she was an orphan. Forced to live with her aunt and uncle, although wonderful people, she was an orphan living in someone else's home. The husband she picked was also an orphan abandoned by his father at an early age and left with a mother that struggled to "make ends meet." Dad's mother died when he was in the service at a ripe age of seventeen. The short span of 18-20 years when all my parents' family were in the home was too short for a vital young woman that soaked up every moment of family life that she thirsted for in her formative years. Suddenly, that cherished time was over.

She ends her poem of loneliness by going to her God believing in the hope of eternal life where Revelation declares that" God will wipe every tear."

The next poem seems to be one that equilibrates her mood of the previous one with the misnomer title of "Happiness." "Remember" is one that looks back on her family life with her husband. She becomes more resolved, more happy, and appreciative of the memories stored. The memories become blessings and not a reminder of relationships lost. That is a promise of Christ to lighten the burden of your yoke. Grace is given by realizing "as long as we live, memories like these will forever be."

Remember

Memories are like silver and gold,
They become more precious as we grow old.
Keep all the good memories in your heart.
Let not the bad memories have any part.

There will become a day in time
A husband or wife will be left behind.
All those memories we have stored away
Will help carry us through our sad days.

Remember our long walks in the park,
The day we listened to the meadow lark,
When we held our baby for the first time,
And watched our children draw their first valentine.

On Christmas night we worked for hours
Putting together a train and water tower.
I finished making a little doll's dress.
That night we got so very little rest.

Early the next morning we were wide awake,
Acted excited about Santa for the children's sake.
How happy we were around the Christmas tree.
As long as we live, memories like these will forever be.

Follow Me

Come take my hand and follow me.
We shall see the beauty of this great land.
We shall travel to the deep blue sea.
There we shall walk in the cool white sand.

Come take my hand and follow me.
We shall climb the mountains high.
We shall look down on the swaying trees,
There we shall watch the great eagles fly.

Come take my hand and follow me.
We shall travel back over ocean, land, and trees.
Through this journey you and I shall see,
The best place to be is home with a loving family.

After Sweet Adeline and her husband were married they did not go beyond the borders of Kansas and Missouri for the rest of their life. Mom did not verbalize the desire to go anywhere, but Dad yearned to go on a train trip through the Rocky Mountains. Their only "vacations" were travels to see relatives that resided in Missouri. In fact, in all the years of their marriage they never once took a "vacation" even to go to the Lake of the Ozarks (an extremely popular place to at least get away for a day or two). They never stayed in any hotels, motels, or campsites.

On those short trips to relatives on the other side of the state, we ate packed lunches or stopped at a grocery store for bread, lunch meat and sodas.

So she says to her husband in her poem "Follow Me" to "take my hand and follow me" as if she is on a demonstrative trip to show her husband what the conclusion would be-- "and you shall see the best place to be is home with a loving family."

I do not remember them eating in a restaurant until, as grown children, we took them out for birthdays or anniversaries. Those restaurant outings were always a joy to the siblings and me to see our parents partake of that event. They enjoyed it despite sweet Adeline feeling a little bit guilty in having money spent on them.

In the defense of my siblings, our parents declined, decisively, being taken by us on any vacation, with or without accompanying grandchildren. Now read her poem "My Hometown" and get another reinforcement of this retrospection.

My Hometown

I live in and love my hometown.
I never vacation the year round.
I love to hear the old familiar sounds.
I enjoy watching the evening sun go down.

When I take my daily walks,
When old friends I often meet,
We love to stop and have a talk.
To me, it's such a refreshing treat.

I know my neighbors by their first names.
There I go to talk about the daily news,
Or maybe just play a few card games,
Or just listen to their points of views.

Yes, I love my hometown, it's true.
This is where I want to spend my days.
I have no desire for something new.
My hometown is where I want to stay.

As I sit in my hotel resort room watching my wife and children prepare for bed my mind wanders back to my childhood and I search my memory banks for an equivalent experience that my children are having. I do not remember a single instance when we had a family vacation other than an extremely rare overnight stay at a relative's house for a single night. (For you readers to know, these retrospections were written over a twenty-year span usually when I was attending continued education courses for my dental licensure, so I left some of the redundancy of the retrospections stand.)

I do not remember a single time in a motel or hotel room with my parents. Yes, we had a few Sunday get aways and I remember some special big hit movies we attended as a family. Nor do I remember anytime my parents dropped us off at a friend's house for a quick escape—even for an evening.

Now I sit in my den and read my words above to finish this small retrospection. I just have finished preparing to teach a Sunday school lesson on the topic "sacrificial love." I wrote in my lesson plans a directive to the class: "Relate how your parents or your spouse has demonstrated sacrificial love." I guess I can take to the class an example. Our current society urges us to stockpile our reserves and manipulate our time schedule so we can obtain leisure time for our personal benefit. My parents realized that fulfillment in life does not come through self-gratification but from giving of themselves and their resources. They found their joy and gratification through sacrificial love—specifically leisure time and a chance to be together. I do not know what kept their emotional and spiritual tanks full—somewhere they found sources for refueling. I know my success has been a source of their joy and I have been conscious and protective of that since early high school. Some of my success can be attributed to a strong effort not to fail—for their sake.

My children have been to countless restaurants and have eaten countless meals outside of the home. They have been on a few nice vacations. I hope my children grasp the concept of sacrificial love—and I think they do. Our always pleasant vacations are building other relationship values for my children; however, each vacation brings this reminder of my parents sacrifice of their leisure time.

Chapter Three

THE LEAN YEARS

Aunt Annabel and her husband, Bob, provided a stable, loving family relationship for Adeline. She had endured many losses of relationships up to the time she was taken in by them, but the stability of her aunt's family was probably the single best long-term event in Adeline's childhood. Annabel's daughter became a little sister to her, and they enjoyed a good relationship for the rest of their lives. Adeline was able to grow up in a modest income family that had a high value for education. Bob had a degree in agriculture and was associated with a state college that allowed Adeline to attend a lab school through high school—except for one more separation that Adeline had to endure.

Bob was asked to take over the teaching position in a very small high school that lost their ag teacher through his death. Adeline was separated from all her friends in the critical Senior year. The whole family moved to this little town, so she was not separated from her foster family, but compounded with all other separations she had to endure, the trauma could have created rebellion. It did not. She graduated, but as many did in those days, it stimulated her to go out on her own upon graduation.

After graduation she left for Kansas City for a technical course in photography and was able to simultaneously secure a job in a huge Katz drug store in the camera and film developing department. She made friends with another young girl, and they became apartment roommates. The relationship turned into a lifelong friendship. Adeline's brother was discharged from the Navy and he, too, became a resident of Kansas City.

Then something wonderful happened. A freshly discharged, good looking sailor came into the store and bought a three-cent stamp from her cashier's spot. They exchanged a few nervous bits of weather commentary. There was a little subtle flirting and the sailor left. The next day the same ex-sailor came in to buy another stamp. The weather was discussed again even though it had not changed from the day before. More subtle two-way flirting occurred.

Now this sailor must have had quite a bit of correspondence because on the third day he returned to buy a third stamp. Each time it was a few minutes after five o'clock; she thought that was a good sign. Adeline guessed he must have a job—close by. He did not wear a ring; he was always alone; so she guessed he had no wife—and maybe no girlfriend. This time the conversation moved to a suspicious topic; it was about the new movie playing up the street. It turned out this ex-sailor had not seen the movie. Neither had Adeline seen the movie. So the conversation ended with the decision that they would both take in the movie that Saturday night. But Adeline had one condition that they would double date with her roommate, Bethany, and her date.

She rushed home to convince both Bethany and her brother to go with them that Saturday night. Apparently it worked because this led to Bethany and Tom getting married later down the timeline.

Eventually, this ex-sailor felt he had a big enough collection of stamps and in a few months later popped the big question as if some of that stamp glue was still stuck to his tongue. Tom and Bethany stood up with them. Eleven months later the author of these words came into the world and was greeted by three people— my mother, a dad that stayed with my mother till her death and an aunt that competed for my attention with my mother. My uncle lost the attention of my aunt. Tom and Bethany were separated in a few months. My mother was never separated from family for the rest of her life!

My Husband . . . Gilbert

There is great peace and joy in having a husband
  that is true.
My dear, this from you, I have had all life through.
In all our life together you have never left me to be alone.
Through the years, my dear, you have made our
  house a home.

There is something extra nice in all you do for me.
In many, many ways you have let me be so free.
In all my hopes and plans you play the greatest part.
For you, my love, are the nearest and dearest to my
  heart.

To me you have shown your love in so many ways.
I look forward to seeing you at the end of each day.
Down deep in my heart I will always cherish you.
Thank you, my dear, for the countless things you do.

I know you have accepted my faults and my ways.
I will thank you for this for the rest of my days.
May we continue to go hand in hand down life's path.
I pray our faith, health, and love will always last.

May some of my loving words stay with you, in
    your heart.
In my life may I always be a precious part.
Thank you for wiping away many of my tears.
Because of you in my life, I have had many less fears.

May life always bring you an abundance of happiness.
For in my thoughts and heart you deserve the very
    best.
May God always keep you in His loving care.
When you need me, my dear, may I always be there.

My dad had a love for trains. For the first six years of their marriage they had no car. Stores and work were very close to an old two-story home they bought. For entertainment, Dad bought model railroad kits and put together railroad cars and side buildings. He filled one room with his model trains. At the end of their sixth year of marriage he sold all that he had amassed, and he was able to buy a good used car. And my sister got a bedroom! The following was a poem written to Gilbert and signed by Mom.

Memories

A boy waited by the railroad tracks
Looking for that old train to come back.
Then he heard it's clickety clack
When he laid his ear on the railroad track.

He ran to the top of the hill,
Its distant whistle was a thrill,
Watching it gliding through the waving grass.
Standing there like a little soldier as it passed.

It was like an old friend as he waved goodbye.
It almost brought tears to his eyes
When that old train disappeared around the bend.
Its clickety clack seem to say, "I'll be back again."

To Gilbert,
Love, Adeline

Adeline and Gilbert have been married for over fifty-one years as of this retrospection (they had been married for sixty -two years when Sweet Adeline passed). I have known them for fifty of those years and I cannot remember a night that they have been apart except for a two-week period that his job took him away. It bothered him so much, he resigned from the job. No other time do I remember even a single night away. So that line was literally fulfilled for Dad, "in your life may I always be a precious part." There were no hunting trips, no all-male retreats, or even overnight business trips. When one had to go, the other did also.

Even within this constant companionship, my mother was free. If she desired to be alone or go somewhere, that decision would have been hers to make. She simply had no desires to go without her husband. She recognizes this in her line "In many, many ways you have let me be so free."

They reached all major decisions as a team, but Mom was the ultimate decision maker in the areas of finance. Dad could and did campaign for and win many elective purchases. However, the family accountant was Mom. Perhaps my mother should oversee the national debt, because she could always balance hers—despite poor income and pressure from us all. Deficit spending was not in her paradigm. This should be a good lesson for many of today's over extended families. Like the old joke: My wife (husband) had plastic surgery . . . I cut up her (his) credit card! That should be used more often. The average credit card debt of young families is completely out of reason.

It is gratifying that a woman that has been with the same man for over fifty years would take the time to express in words her love for her husband. She expresses her thanks, her shortcomings, and her faithfulness. She prays for these things to last. Three things that no philosopher, no wiser person, no clergyman could top. What would be the three most important things that a loving couple would pray to last? My mother is well down the road on her theological journey and well developed in her marital relationship. She prays our "faith, health, and love will last." In other retrospections I comment on their meager existence on social security in an old house.

But I realize here, their riches are not so much worldly as they are spiritual.

We never had a house that had an attic where items were stored—especially toy chests full of old memorable toys. This fact did not keep mother from using her poetic license to express her real memories when cleaning out old toyboxes. Mothers give away old toys that are not used anymore by their children. In those days toys were more durable and could be passed on to relatives with children a little younger. Special toys were put away and stored if they had special meanings to the child or parent. Special Christmas toy gifts were more likely to be saved. After we were married for twelve years we had our first child. Before we knew the gender of that child I had a toy gift from Mom. It was two of my cast metal toy truck and trailers. One had a log hauling trailer and the other had a cattle hauling trailer. The paint was literally worn off the cattle trailer door where I put plastic animals in through the back doors. Often I would put a pet cat in and haul them around pretending to haul a lion to a city zoo.

My two children, both girls, were not interested in playing with them. The toys are displayed on top of my bookshelves in my library. I was glad they did not want to play with them; they are my trucks! Now my two grandsons are petitioning me to get them down so they may play with them. So I will. Consider now the "Toy Chest Memories" that we siblings have pieces of the collection. Boys never outgrow toys. Our toys just get bigger and more expensive.

Toy Chest of Memories

While rummaging through the attic one rainy day,
I came upon the old forgotten toy chest.
I carefully brushed away the dust,
A little mildew and from the handles some rust.

Looking down I saw items of joy and memories.
I could see the past life excerpts so clear.
I took my hand and slowly brushed away
An emotional, joyful, pleasant little tear.

A little rag doll with tousled hair,
A wooden train pulled by a string,
A staunch little soldier dressed in blue,
And a singular tarnished golden ring.

Each little toy held its own memories.
If they could speak, oh, the stories they could tell.
How they were loved by the children in play
And how, even in fun, they were cared for so well.

How quickly the years have come and gone.
But for as long as they and theirs shall be.
There will forever always be bits
And grace placed pieces of me.

I would stare at the picture in my fourth grade reading book for minutes at a time. Frequently going back to that page long after the lesson was covered, I dreamed that that could be my family's home. The picture showed, by today's standards, a starkly simple kitchen. An old white refrigerator with the electrical unit on top—a unit that was out of date even at that time—sat beside a wall and in front a simple, gray-painted table with a wooden chair.

A gingham red and white tablecloth covered the tabletop. A young boy with books just came in from school through the back door and was greeted by his mother peeling apples for a pie that would be the desert for that night's supper. The mother had a shirtwaist dress on like my mother wore, but the woman was different. This mother stayed at home and was a housewife. The father, not in the picture, was obviously at work and would be home at 5:30 to have dinner at 6:00. I am sure the little sister was in the other corner of the kitchen not shown in the picture. She would be playing with her dolls.

Upstairs would be the boy's bedroom with a big model airplane hanging from the ceiling lamp fixture. There would be a desk in the corner where the boy could draw pictures of army tanks and store his baseball cards.

The house would actually have a front and back yard— probably with a white picket fence in front. There would be an apple tree and another tree with a tire swing in it. All of this could surely be seen by anyone who looked at that textbook picture long enough.

My father and mother fulfilled all my needs. My mother made dozens of apple pies and greeted me cheerfully when I arrived home from school. We had a better refrigerator and a bigger table than was in that textbook picture. However, I knew that the rest of the house, not depicted in that photograph, was not attached to a general store that robbed me of frequent intervals of time with my mother. Not just after school, but throughout the evening. That store constantly invaded our life robbing my parents of any sustained rest, any sustained moments with their children and any sustained time with each other.

Our living room was separated only via a small door from the store. Cigar smoke, laughter, boisterous talk all leaked into our family chamber perpetually piercing our privacy. Like a butler responding to the master's ring, the bell on the door would summon a parent from their children interrupting Chinese checkers, card games, or TV.

What was truly remarkable was the moments of time my parents did squeeze in with my siblings and me. I have played countless games of checkers and Chinese checkers with both of my parents. I remember watching certain TV shows regularly, but I do not remember a constant diet of it. I am not sure if my father ever got to watch a full half-hour of the Red Skelton show. Perhaps they knew it was too difficult to start books or other projects and found it time consuming, as well as, beneficial to play those board and card games with their children. At least I did not play any cards in college! That social collegiate need was satisfied and that probably saved a lot of study time. Perhaps those frequent interruptions developed a tenacity within my parents to keep playing those annoying boardgames to keep them in our demand for their attention. Intuitively, they must have sensed the invasion.

My pre-teen years did not know that front yard with an apple tree and the picket fence. But it did know a set of parents that provided increments of time for their children through their long hours in that general store. Is not it odd that after years go by you forget those times your parents said "no" to something that you just had to do, or the earth would come to a grinding halt—a response that welted up an intense emotional wave. The temper of time shapes the metal of our esteem, and we remember the subtle nurturing parental performances. I wonder what effect on my self-esteem would have resulted if those numerous board games with my parents were removed from the nurturing equation.

To My Daughter

Dear daughter I was thinking of you today,
The things you have done for me along the way.
If I had a million you could have a part,
It would be a gift straight from the heart.

I would like to plant an oak tree
With lots of love to you from me
To make shade for you someday,
When I have gone so very far away.

As its autumn leaves begin to fall
Remember love is the best gift of all.
As time and life quickly passes by
The time will come when I shall die.

As you walk through the colorful leaves,
Look at all the beautiful colors of me.
Stop for a moment and you shall hear
A beautiful songbird so very near.

When you see little birds up in the trees
Just stop to say "hi" and think of me.
Keep all the good memories in your heart.
In your life I pray they will become a precious part.
Love, Mom

There is a special connection between a mother and her daughter that any male would be hard pressed to explain. Maybe I should go back and edit that first sentence and insert an adjective of "spiritual" before the term "connection." Why? It seems that in this era "motherhood" is being diluted—but that is a sermon for another time.

My mother had a special bond with her daughter and her gifts to her were "straight from the heart." This poem was written in her latter life just before Alzheimer's when my parents were carefully managing their meager retirement funds. Mom was a true sacrificial giver and always had a sense of regret she could not give more. She states she would like to plant an oak tree in her daughter's honor. My sister understands her symbolism.

Mom's greatest joy in nature were trees and birds. I helped her plant several trees in my childhood, and she would always comment on how the tree would be a legacy and a remembrance of her as I got older. That, I am sure, was shared with my sister. Elsewhere in these retrospections will be a commentary on her poem of the weeping willow tree.

Mom so loved birds that she developed an uncanny ability to imitate bird songs through whistling. It was a frequent source of displayed joy requested by her children and grandchildren. A whistling grandmother is, indeed, a rare find.

Her daughter was very much aware of Sweet Adeline's love of trees and birds. This poem is a deeply symbolic outpouring of Mom's love for her daughter. She wanted to give a gift that would be perpetual in my sister's consciousness. I believe it is

It turns out that the male siblings did not merit a poem like her daughter. Perhaps her love was held back until we granted her grandchildren. Both Don and I had children later in our timelines. None-the-less the story of my brother's arrival tells something of Sweet Adeline's character, so here goes the retrospection of brother Don—poem or not!

"It is probably nothing. I will go into Maysville and let Dr. Crawly check me out." Mom told Dad.

So, she took the car and drove nine miles into town leaving Dad to work the General store. It was one of two stores in the town of Oak; population was eleven. It was one of the last of its kind, a true general store. We bought cream, old worn-out hens, and eggs. We sold gas, tires, hardware, livestock feed and a few groceries. The hours were long, from seven in the morning to nine at night. The customers came there for talk as much as for their goods. Mom was a good talker and Dad was a good listener. Both were gentle people—so gentle that credit was given too often and for too much. A large rack of charge pads, each with a name of a family boldly written on the binding, sat beside the cash register. Patrons would "charge" their purchases and settle monthly or whenever they would get around to it. That burgeoning rack became the downfall of the simple business. There were no giants like Visa or Mastercard to absorb the losses from the deadbeats. This was a true "Mom and Pop" store. Credit cards, better cars and larger stores killed these little meeting places that gave an area a sense of community. I cannot help from feeling that America lost a lot of its inner strength when these places died out. It was a place for networking to occur before anyone knew what networking was. People shared their problems, dreams, and successes at these little markets. Everyone knew everyone's business and probably people were a little more careful because of it.

Mom started for town thinking that just a routine exam would end in her returning to the store to complete her 14-hour day. Little did she know that she would give birth to her third child and leave Dad, my six-year-old sister and me stranded at the store with no way to retrieve her and our new family member. We had only one oil-burning, smoke producing Plymouth for transportation. In the special delivery room that was nothing more than a little bedroom with a few medical looking charts and stainless-steel fixtures, Mom gave birth to Donald, a blond seven-pound, three-ounce boy. No complications, no anesthesia, and no insurance—fee for the whole pregnancy monitoring and delivery, $300! That was the simple way my not so simple brother came into the world.

Dad always paid his bills, even though many of his customers did not pay him. Dad would take all silver dollars that would come through the store and drop them in a crock. Silver dollars were still in circulation on an infrequent rate, but not rare. He paid Dr. Crawly's fee with three hundred of them. They never made it to the bank. Dr Crawly kept them for his commonly known collection. I wonder what they would be worth today?

We did not leave Mom in that room behind Doc Crawly's office. Our grand great aunt "Nana" came to our rescue in her new Oldsmobile and took Dad to Maysville to retrieve Mom and the new Don.

In contrast to some of the diluted concepts of contemporary psychology that try to diminish the uniqueness of what "female" means, attached to those "x" chromosomes are a deep sense of nurturing that is shared over an invisible network connecting spiritual mothers. So I speak of the mothers that consciously engage parenting principles that develop God's universal morality in their children. It is nearly like the network of the root system of the Aspen pine trees that become like one functioning organism.

A mother's reward highly prized is seeing their own perceived good aspects duplicated in their children. Even greater value of that reward is reaped when the mother sees that same value transferred to their grandchildren by their child's parenting. These subtle increments of joy spring up unexpectantly and are the results of God's grace.

If the unexpectant increment that pops up is a result of Satan's evil, it seems to bring up, outwardly at least, deeper emotional response to mothers. The bombing of the governmental building in Oklahoma City, Oklahoma, had a distinct impact on Sweet Adeline. Her emotional response was triggered by that deep innate sense of motherhood's shared loss. Like the predictability of a mechanical clock her next tick-tock was the emotional movement of her mind to the time of the Lord symbolized by "the empty swings that sway in the wind." The loss is deeply felt but the "why" cannot be fully understood and to cope for Sweet Adeline was to write out her grief and rely on an omniscient God.

Precious Lives

There is a silent empty playground
Where children used to laugh and play.
Now we only hear their haunting sounds
As we remember their yesterdays.

The crying wind is like human wails
As the empty swings are swaying in the wind,
Like deserted lonely ships without a sail
To bring them to their journey's end.

Precious little lives were taken away
By a heartless terrorist's hand
While little children were at play
In that Oklahoma City land.

Sadness lives within their homes.
Children's sounds no longer to hear.
Where fathers and mothers feel so alone
And memories only bring sad tears.

Our Father gathered precious buds that day.
They will all bloom in heaven in His time
To make His beautiful heavenly bouquet.
They're safe in loving arms; do not weep or pine.

Chapter Four

THE SILENCE OF THE EMPTY NEST

Sweet Adeline anticipated her forced empty nest years and turned to her discipleship for strength. Don, the last child, was eight years after me, Linda was only two years younger than me. Linda was first to give her a singular granddaughter, but grandchildren did not come fast enough for Sweet Adeline. My first came twelve years into marriage and Don had years before marriage and children. That was a long time for an anticipating grandmother.

She entered a period focused on developing close friendships with her God and with God-fearing women. She focused her poetry around expressing her beliefs and describing her relationships with other women closest to her. She expanded into writing things for the church women's group.

My father was a poor carpenter, but he was not afraid to tackle anything. The result was generally functional, but the esthetics were always lacking. Dad could tell that mom was enjoying her writing hobby and needed a distraction from family separation.

To give Mom some special space for her writing and to house the computer, hard drive, and printer provided by her sons, Dad decided to add on a little nook to the back of the house adjacent to the kitchen. It was a project from which they both got enjoyment. A few bushes and some roses hid most of the architectural faux pas. The interior was decorated based on their joys and interests. Dad had a television, a few model train engines, and a few other train nick-nacks. Mom's side was taken up by her computer and printer. The whole wall space on Mom's side was occupied by pictures of birds—except a space in the middle for two special pictures—Jesus Christ and Marcus Allen. Marcus was in his Kansas City Chiefs uniform.

The whole family learned not to call on Sunday mornings because they were in church; it was useless to call during game time, because they would not answer the phone. No family pictures adorned that wall. Only Jesus Christ and Marcus Allen were worthy!

A Shadow of Me

When you have gone many miles away,
May happiness be yours from day to day.
May all things beautiful be yours to see.
There by your side will be a shadow of me.

As you look upon the beauty of the sunrise,
May there always be a rainbow in your sky.
As you gaze upon the awesomeness of a majestic tree,
There by your side will be a shadow of me.

May the warmth of the sunshine always embrace you.
May you be surrounded with love all life through.
As the crystal waters continue to run into the sea,
There by your side will be a shadow of me.

May God keep you in his tender care.
My love for you will always be there.
Of sorrow and loneliness may you always be free.
There by your side will be a shadow of me.

If by chance I should be missed,
My dear friend, just do this.
Just look by your side and you will see,
There will always be a shadow of me.

My mother was always kind and friendly to everyone. She is the incarnate "Good Samaritan." If you recall your Bible stories the good Samaritan saw to it that the beaten man was cared for but did not remain for accolades. Mom was like that. When the helping deed was done, she did not remain for praises. It was simply done in the normal course of her life. She interacted with many people, but closeness came guarded. She usually had one or two close friends at a time as if her attention went elsewhere she would be cheating her closest friend. That friend would be kept until separation came through one moving with their family away to a new location as many did in her life.

This is probably why she starts her poem with "when you have gone many miles away." Periodically, we would see old friends from the past and all came back out of true friendship for a visit. The old friends seem to sense that "if by chance I should be missed, my dear friend, just do this; just look by your side and you will see there will always be a shadow of me." The visits were always well accepted, and it seemed that her friends could just restart where they left off.

I find myself a little like that, as well. I seem to develop a few singular strong friendships within my broader circle of friends. These special friends are friends for life, and I still call and visit them. These friends seem to be anchors to my past in each phase of my life and I, too, feel like beside them are shadows of me. True, reciprocating friendship is the most important and satisfying relationship there is. I learned the value for long-term friendship through my mother's example. And like my mother, my friends are diverse without pattern except for the characteristic of loyalty. Hmm...

Now read about a close friendship that developed in my mother's fifties. I probably saw more laughter in their relationship than any other. They simply seemed to have more fun than other pairings.

My Friend---To Shirley with Love

We are together, my friend, no matter how far apart.
I loved you, my friend, almost from the start.
I did not buy you; God gave you to me, my friend.
I will cherish and keep you to the very end.

Thank you for loving, caring, and accepting my ways.
Thank you for giving me a part of your life each day.
I value your friendship more than silver or gold.
My love for you can never be taken, given, or sold.

I remember all the good times, laughter, and tears.
Thank you for helping to fade away some of my fears.
Thank you for filling an empty space in my heart.
In my life you will always be a precious part.

Thank you for being honest, dependable, and fair.
For me, I know how much you really care.
Thank you for the close moments we do share.
For in my heart they will always be there.

A friend is as a soft, gentle breeze on a summer's day.
A friend can shed light in your path in many,
    many ways.
A true friend is as pure and beautiful as the
    falling snow.
Being together without a word spoken, a friend will
    know.

How sad to live without a special friend.
In life, some never find one even to the very end.
Again, I must say I am very thankful for you.
Forgive me for my faults and the thoughtless
    things I do.

Thank you for understanding my off ways.
Thank you for helping me through those sad days.
Thank you for all the many little things untold.
Your friendship is a very precious gift to hold.

Down life's path may our friendship continue to grow.
May we share our life and live it as we go.
May we always be faithful, forgiving, honest and
    true.
May we always treasure what we have all life through.

Sweet Adeline did not reveal to me the identity of this next friend recognized by her poetic effort. Several hints in her poem causes me to fix on one friend of over fifty years. She speaks of pictures taken; my interpretation are physical pictures taken during and after her photography course. Young women of those days, without cars in an urban area, took walks for enjoyment and to go to grocery stores. Without TVs in those beginning years they had time for "fulfilling talks."

She speaks of years apart, but old fashion letter writing was an oft used means of communication like texting and emailing is today. Her letters to and from this friend covered nearly a half century. She valued and mentioned old remembrances— "I remember long ago most of all."

Why she did not try to visit such a friend is an enigma

to me since this friend lived less than two hours' drive away. My clairvoyance suggests to me it was the friend's wishes relative to her current family situation.

As alluded to before, writing these poems was a method to cope with unpleasant or disappointing things, a method to extend love, and a method to exercise creativity. When I asked her directly why she did not make an effort to see this very close friend of her early adult years, she gave me an answer like a politician that evades a direct press question. The last line is revealing to me without further comment from me: "I just wanted to say I love you, and goodbye my friend." One last observation. Of all the reunions of old friends in later years, all of them came to her. She never asked her husband, to my knowledge, to go seek a visitation.

My Friend

When I awoke this morning I thought of you
And of all the things we used to do.
When autumn leaves began to fall,
I remember long ago most of all.

As the colored leaves skip across the ground,
Yet all things lie in silent sound,
When so many memories fill my mind,
I try and only keep the happy kind.

I think often of our long walks
And our long fulfilling talks.
All the pictures we took along the way,
They are my treasure to this day.

There were many years we were apart.
My dear, I carried you in my heart.
If my life should suddenly come to an end,
I just wanted to say, I love you and goodbye my friend.

Take My Hand

Dear God, do you care and love me still,
Knowing all the good deeds I should have done,
The countless things I do against your will,
For you, the souls I should have won?

When I neglect to go to those in despair,
When I proceed to go my selfish way,
Not wanting to be burdened with their care,
Finding excuses to do for them another day?

When I let the daily news disturb my heart and
    mind,
And find myself drifting into a state of fear,
When I do not take the Bible and find
Peace, tranquility and you, dear God, so near?

When I am in doubt of things you have said,
Will I have been in question too long,
Will I rise in glory after I am dead?
Will I get to hear the beautiful heavenly songs?

Forgive me for the thoughtless things I do.
Dear God, I cannot make it on my own.
Hold my hand tightly, and I will follow you,
For I am so very weak and cannot walk alone.

I am humbled by the clarity of her question of God, "Do you care and love me still, when I neglect to go to those in despair, when I proceed my selfish way?" This is a woman who has spent her whole lifetime helping others. Neither of my parents could say "no" to anyone. My thoughts go back to several examples. At the time, it seemed so natural and was done without fanfare that only when I read my mother's verse in my middle years do I realize the depth of their giving nature.

At the South side of our general store setting about 150 feet away was a two-room building that was probably no more than 450 square feet. It did not have running water, therefore no bathroom. It was cleaned up, painted and prepared for a woman who was having some type of marital and financial problems. She was pregnant.

She lived there for a while, probably at no expense. When she got on her feet, had her baby, and who I assumed was the father of the child returned, they departed. My parents were happy and relieved but spoke little about the couple's problem.

That two-room building was occupied for a while by my grandfather Floyd. He was a long-time widower, out of work and, of course, out of money. He did some odd jobs. Helped my parents around the store and ate at our table. Time passed and he left to essentially care for our aging bachelor relatives trying to end their days on an old farm.

A new highway was constructed that passed by our store and the building was setting on the new highway right of way. It had to be moved or tore down. It was sold to a local farmer, and they moved it away. Probably for the best, because the only income that building gave my folks was the near give away price my parents got from the farmer.

"Not wanting to be burdened with their care, finding excuses to do for them another day?" Givers always feel a little guilty because they always feel they could have done more. This guilt is compounded when their effort tires them, and they feel burdened. My parents were mistaking fatigue for guilt!

Later they sold the general store and tried the life of a school janitor and a school cafeteria cook. After the transitions, all bills were paid, and a "new" house was purchased that required lots of repairs. They sold that repaired house and got a decent older home with a few acres of land. My sister and I graduated from high school living in that old house that had ample room for us. Then what did they do? They returned to their giving ways.

The recipient of several trips to the doctor, several trips to the church ladies meeting and trips to various work functions of the church were enjoyed by a blind lady that was an amazing worker, but without transportation during the daytime hours when her husband was working. Guess who volunteered many times for that function?

This helping of the downtrodden continued when they moved to a neighboring school district that recruited both of them to lead their janitorial and cooking staffs. The house they bought at this time was the house they remained in till the nursing home. The house to the East was a big old two-story fire trap that needed a lot of maintenance and repair. An older woman lived there and apparently had no family in the area. Mom befriended her and my parents cleaned up the yard, hauled off the trash. They gave her an older functional refrigerator they were using and bought a new one for themselves because "it was time to replace it" as an excuse to us adult offspring for their actions.

Over the years the old lap siding was covered with rolled roofing by my father in areas where the siding was literally falling off the house. My father patched the roof again and again. The old furnace went out and the elderly, poor woman living there was slowly going blind and probably slowly killing herself with a kerosene portable stove set up in the kitchen to keep herself from freezing.

The old woman was taken to the doctor, taken to the grocery store and watched over. I am not sure how often my parents paid their elderly neighbor's bills, but I don't believe my parents "proceeded to go their selfish way."

The old woman is gone, and the old house is gone. As I write this retrospection in my fifties the oldest house in that block is now my parents' home. Time has quietly passed with their ability to physically care for their own home. How foreign it must felt for them to be in their seventies and not be able to climb the ladders with the roofing and paint brush in hand. How restricting it must had been for them to be even more severely limited with their only source of income being a meager monthly social security check and pension from the school. How sad it was for a couple so giving in their productive years to be forced to be on the receiving side of the equation.

An unprecedented, but brief, burst of tears came when my mother told me their roof started to leak and she couldn't do anything about it . . . blessed are the meek.

My mother asks, "will I rise in glory when I am dead?"

I believe the answer is yes. Their countless acts of giving were done in the highest circumstance—without fanfare, without expectations of return, and without hesitation. And I might add, without their children even being aware that a strong example was being added to their value system.

Sweet Adeline again asks her Father, in the poem "Our Father," if He will accept her in heaven when she fails to do all the work she has been exposed to in His service. This is the heart of a servant.

The poem "Struggling" follows next and, again, reveals her heart as a servant in another way. In her mind she dreams the recipient is thankful and appreciative. Don't we often dream this whenever we give unabashedly. This dream expressed in the last two lines of the poem is the servant's way of rewarding themselves. Its why a giver keeps on giving. It's a self-inflicted reward.

Our Father

Be with us our heavenly Father.
Forgive us from day to day.
May you give us strength to serve you
In kindness and in a loving way.

May we do our best each day,
For our tomorrow may never be.
Will you claim us for your own?
To be with you in your heavenly home?.

When we stand before you dear Savior
Knowing all the work we failed to do,
Will we approach you in fear and shame?
If so, we only have ourselves to blame.

Then it will be too late for tears.
Our opportunities shall be no more.
For things we should have done or said
For our earthly life is past and dead.

Struggling

I saw a struggling little vine in the crack of a wall.
I carefully removed it and planted it in my garden.
I watered and cared for the little vine each day.
It became quite beautiful in the late fall.

I saw a little boy pale and hungry by a garden wall.
His dark eyes seem to reach into my very soul.
Daily I returned and fed the little dark eyed boy.
He grew to be quite tall by the late fall.

The days went by, and he was no longer there.
I often thought of the little dark eyed boy.
I returned many times to the garden wall.
But he was not to be found anywhere.

I returned to the wall years later feeling blue.
There stood a handsome man straight and tall.
His dark eyes seem to reach into my very soul
As he took my hand and said, "I will always
   love you."

The next poem is written on an oft used moral principle that is summarized by the old saying, "never judge the book by its cover." But many times we can judge the book by its cover or title. So, we learn by our experience.

Mom takes the old moral and slaps the face of the flippant Christian congregant on several layers of meaning. Mom practiced what she preached. She helped many of the downtrodden she came across as described in the preceding retrospections. She was critical of this type of prejudice when displayed in her church. We use church many times as a sanctuary from the secular world for ourselves and when the unclean in body and spirit invades our sanctuary, we tend to ignore or pull back from that intruder. We promptly forget the acronym that most Christians are familiar--WWJD. We fail to act like Jesus when someone violates the status quo of our pristine pews. My mother would not be the type that would go up and give him a hug, but she would be one of the first to speak to an outsider and invite him back. On subsequent visits, I would wager that she would start up a conversation with the man. She would also be the first to realize the lesson if this incident occurred in her congregation. Proof you say? The woman she sheltered in the small building and the neighbor she kept from starving as described in the previous retrospections are just two representative examples.

Where Is Our Love?

There was a man who no one paid any attention to
With his dirty old jeans that were faded blue
There he was in church every Sunday
Never in the collections did he give any money.

He sat in the pew in the very back
By his side was his dirty old backpack.
The air around him was very stale
Many times he would look very pale.

Everyone seemed to avoid this man
Never did anyone shake his hand
One Sunday he was not in the pew in the back,
With his worn and dirty old backpack.

Most everyone seemed so very much relieved.
He will never be back they all hoped and believed.
Next Sunday to church came a well-dressed man.
Everyone hurried to shake his hand.

He was invited to sit near the front.
He was even invited out to lunch.
He quietly sat down in the pew in the back
By his side he placed an old worn-out backpack.

A Rose in the Snow

Hello my dear
I just came to visit you today
I have a few things to tell you though
First of all I miss you so.

The ground is fluffy white with snow,
With beautiful flakes falling softly down
I remember how you loved the snow
Especially when it was not so very cold.

Our children are doing very well.
We are grandparents once again.
A beautiful little girl
With big blue eyes and blond curls.

The willow tree we planted
Almost four years ago
Has grown to be quite tall
Remember we had such a beautiful fall.

I finished the rose garden
We started so long ago.
You gathered me such beautiful stones
And you did it for me all alone.

Our friends still come and go.
Appreciate them so very much
They help me through my sad days
Since the angels came and took you away.

I know how much you love roses.
I visited our favorite florist shop
And bought you a big red rose.
I'll just lay it here in the snow.

The snow is still softly falling
I must go and say goodbye for now.
Time seems to be slipping away
It is almost the end of another day.

I will be back and visit you again.
No one will ever take your place.
I thank you so much my dear
For your precious love through the years.

Sweet Adeline was typically very sympathetic to her friend's physical and spiritual needs. She readily accommodated their feelings in a sharing way. Instead of trying to encourage her friends to "snap out of it" so to speak, she would join where her friends were, and then help move them out of their grieving.

In her last years in the Alzheimer's unit, she would seem to assess her fellow unit mates and be friends with them, even within their fantasies. I was walking down the halls with her during a visit, and we came upon a patient that was holding an infant doll wrapped in a blanket. As Sweet Adeline approached her, she behaved like one would when coming upon a friend walking her baby.

"Oh, and how is your sweet baby today?" asked Mom as she pulled the blanket back a little to take a peek. "She looks happy, Beverly. You are taking good care of her."

After we passed and got down the hall out of ear shot, Mom looked at me as if she did not want me to be confused and said, "You know . . . that is not a real baby."

She followed this mode of behavior long before Alzheimer's. Because of her ability to assimilate and reflect the emotions of her friends, she would be asked to accommodate friends to the hospital or to the cemetery. One specific friend she drove to the cemetery several times. Mom's creative mind took in her friend's emotions, and she expressed them through her poetry after taking her widow friend to the cemetery one snowy day. She inserted her own preferences into the scenario in the poem, "A Rose in the Snow." She included the things most precious to her. Writers will understand this comment but expressing one's feelings in prose or poetry is a way to release emotions that one collects. It is a way to package emotions, if needed, so one can return to them quickly to re-experience them or share them. It can be a cathartic technique for the author. Perhaps this is what this book is for this author.

Mom loved weeping willow trees and roses. Dad collected rocks and placed them in a cluster for her to fashion a small rose garden. Eventually, all her homes had a weeping willow tree.

The last poem in this grouping expresses her emotional ties with God and nature. Nature is not God; nature is an expression of God's creativity. Sweet Adeline enjoyed her Creator's creativity as a gift of grace to her. Enjoying nature was a way of feeling close to her Creator. As expressed previously, Sweet Adeline especially loved trees and birds. She knew God placed them here for our enjoyment and she believed they would be a part of her physical eternity.

The weeping willow tree was a popular yard tree in the 50's through 70's by my recollection, but has since lost its popularity, by my observation. They had a graceful flowing appearance that blended well with a lot of architectural home designs.

Mom asks, "Did you ever hear the cry of the weeping willow tree?" Strong summer breezes blowing through the dangling branches gives a forlorn sound that drifts through open bedroom windows at night when you are trying to sleep. If the breeze is soft the sound can be sleep-inducing; if the wind blows hard it can mimic the sound of a baby crying. The sound will keep many from falling asleep.

That forlorn sound is a childhood memory reawakened by my mother's poem. I can remember being lulled to sleep whenever the summer breeze was light. When summer storms sneaked in at night the crying sound would wail louder and louder until it would awaken me. If you are in a darker mood, the sound could stimulate an active creative mind to uncomfortable dreams.

I now live in a housing area devoid of large mature trees and devoid of any weeping willow trees. When I pass a housing area and serendipitously sight a weeping willow tree my thoughts, however brief, always passes by a memory of my mother due to her love of that tree, but I don't miss "the cry of the weeping willow tree."

I helped her plant many trees on the grounds of several of her homes. She had a special affinity for weeping willow trees and wrote a poem about that.

The Weeping Willow Tree

Did you ever hear the cry of the willow tree?
It is sad and lonely as can be,
When you hear that cry of the weeping willow tree.

Warm tears will fall from your eyes
Through sadness your mind can see
When you hear that cry of the weeping willow tree.

The willow sways gracefully in the breeze
Peaceful memories get brought back to me
When you lie in the shadow of the weeping willow
tree.

The last poem of this chapter had an odd stimulus for its creation. Sweet Adeline's son-in-law drew her an etching of a bird that had a unique look and pose. That image stimulated a memory or a creative burst that resulted in the poem "The Young Soldier." We know the etching was the stimulus for the poem through her direct statement confirming it. She did not explain her symbolism. You have read about the life and beliefs of Sweet Adeline before her Alzheimer's was significant. So you may take a hand at interpreting the imagery.

The Young Soldier

It was a damp and chilly day
As a young soldier lay in a ditch
With his gun held tightly in his hands,
As he looked over the battle-scarred land.

He knew his buddies were near
From the signals they gave through the night.
He felt this was his duty to do,
And to his country he would be true.

He thought of his wife and baby back home.
How he would love to hold them in his arms.
He could see his mom baking cookies in her kitchen.
He knew his dad was getting ready to go fishin'.

Suddenly the sun began to shine so bright and clear
As he stood up to feel the warmth of the sun.
He saw a little bird perched on a broken limb
Singing so sweetly he knew it was just for him.

Then a sharp crack and a bullet pierced the air.
The young soldier fell to the ground.
For a moment he was back home.
As death came the young soldier was not alone.

The little bird finished singing his song
As if it were only for the young soldier.
Then the bird spread its wings and flew
And the bird disappeared into the sky of blue.

Chapter Five

ALZHEIMER'S, THE LAST ASSAULT OF SATAN

I have read scripture and have read many books on the reflection of scripture, but I am confused with the full spectrum of Satan's power. I do not know his limits, but if Satan had this power and Alzheimer's disease had not been developed, Satan would have created it. It is an evil disease. Clarity alternates with confusion; confidence alternates with reluctance; and memory alternates with a pure state of unawareness. And to make it worse, the victim is sometimes aware of not being aware. They can look upon a person and know that they should know them. Their hearts tell them what their brains cannot. That is the most evil and most cruel portion of the disease that delights Satan; he can use the loss of love and relationship of the victim and family to threaten the family's relationship to their God. Satan's delight.

One evening approaching mid-night I received a call from my mother. Her voice rung more with determination than it did with fear as she told me why she called at a late hour.

"There is a strange man in my bed," she said with a simple tone as if she were telling me there was a strange dog in her yard.

"It's your husband, Gilbert," I assured her.

"No, it's not Gilbert."

I directed her, "Go look at his face and then go into the family room and look at you and Gilbert's anniversary picture hanging on the wall and see if that is the same man." She laid the telephone down indicated by the thud I heard. A few minutes passed.

She came back to the phone and flatly said without emotion, "Its Gilbert." Click . . . dial tone.

Twenty minutes later I got another phone call. This time it was from Adeline's brother, Tom, who lived on the opposite side of the state of Missouri.

"Robert, I got an unusual phone call a few minutes ago from your mother."

"Yes, so did I." I had to break the news to him that his sister's Alzheimer's was now going from periodic symptomology to consistent presence.

Isn't it an evil disease? She could remember my phone number and her brother's phone number without looking it up. She did not have a cell phone, just a simple push button land line phone on the wall in the kitchen. She knew our numbers by memory, but she did not recall the face of her husband of fifty years. Satanic familial evil.

That incident was repeated a couple of times. I think Dad was thankful he did not own a handgun.

As the symptomology continued to increase the periods of lucidity decreased in numbers and duration. Dad assumed the cooking duties and was capable of doing it for a reasonable time. The house was kept far better than most young couples having a family, but less than Mom's standards set over the previous five decades. Dad's sight was declining. He had age related macular degeneration long before it was diagnosed. He was becoming more and more aware of losing his visual acuity.

Mom had taken over driving outside of town for several years before. Dad made a remarkable decision. On a visit to see them he presented the keys to the car to me with only three words of explanation. "I can't see." That was it. Eventually after living by himself for several years and after Mom had passed, he came to me again and said, "I can't see the settings on the cooking stove or the thermostat." He was ready to go to a care facility.

So, for a while we had Dad in his home and Mom in an Alzheimer's unit. She actually did well after a period for adjustment.

The blessing she got from God is she behaved like she was one of the attending staff. I am sure that most of the time she realized she was a resident of the facility, but her servant nature would bleed through, and she adjusted by taking on that well-rehearsed role. She would help people coming and going to lunch, return lost residents wandering in the halls to their rooms, talk with visitors to other residents and brag about how well their loved one was doing.

Let me give you a true anecdote that illustrates the nature of her relationship with the staff.

My younger daughter came home from a day of teaching her kindergartners with a big smile on her face. She is a tenured teacher and frequently has student teachers under her. Also, she is an unofficial leader of the multiple kindergarten teachers informal task group. At an informal meeting including the current student teachers, one of the student teachers said that her sister just had a baby and they named her after a sweet elderly resident of the Alzheimer's unit her nurse-sister worked in. She went on to say, "Everyone, staff and residents alike, loves this woman. She is a constant joy. She had an old-fashioned name that my sister loves. They named their little girl, Adeline."

My daughter followed up with the question, "Where does your sister work?" Some follow up questions confirmed it was our Sweet Adeline! It turned out the grandmother and grandfather of baby Adeline are friends of ours. Grandpa had worked as my dental assistant on multiple mission trips to Jamaica. Small world! That story was a boost to our whole family dealing with Sweet Adeline's decline. Sweet Adeline was still doing her Father's will.

God's Preeminence

Make the best of each of your days.
Use your love in the very best way.
Start each day with a song in your heart.
Do not let annoying little thoughts have any part.

Do not let making money take all your time.
No matter if you do not have a single dime.
Remember to always put God in your life first
And my dear children you will never thirst.

On a visit when I took Dad to see her and after the initial excitement of our presence settled down, we all sat around and had a normal conversation without the presence of our old friend Alzheimer. Oddly, but true to form for a servant receiving calming grace from her God, she started talking about her life there. She told a few short anecdotes about her fellow residents. Then she made this remark.

"I just don't know how much longer I can work here. You know, I am not a spring chicken anymore."

Her whole life was a series of adjustments that she faced head on, especially in her place of domicile. On one plane she probably knew that she was a resident, but on another her engrained discipleship caused her to truly submit to the will of God, accept her position in life, and focused on God. Her poetry and her life are a witness to the assessment above. Consider the short poems that came later in her life.

A Little Bush

If you are just a little bush on the side of a hill,
And not a beautiful tree by the side of the sea,
Then be the best little bush that you can be.

To Be Remembered

The little snowflakes drifted to earth
Only to find they could not last.
To liquid they turned and watered the turf.
Each spring a bit of their being will come to pass.

Longer poems evolved to shorter poems as she approached the time she went to the Alzheimer's unit. I asked and received periodic mailings of her works. Sometimes I would receive a little note that she had rewritten one that "she didn't like." But via multiple requests, I think I have them all. Not all, however, are included in this book. Below are samplings of some of the shorter ones. Some have been slightly edited without changing the poetic attempt. She never dated them, so when they were written within her struggles, I do not know.

Time

The great ocean roars.
The desert wind blows.
The great eagle soars.
Time takes its tolls.

When the ocean becomes dry,
When the desert winds no longer blow
And the great eagle dies,
But forever lives man's soul.

Patience

Apples on a tree.
Grapes on a vine.
Honey made by bees.
Awards come in time.
Just you watch and see,
Leaves don't stay on trees.

The Answer is in You

September rains.
December snows.
What's to gain?
The wind blows.
Hate, love, pain.
We each must grow.
But to remain sane,
Oh! What seeds we sow.
Is life just a game?
The answer is in you, you know!

The foci of Sweet Adeline's poems usually were centered on relationships. She wrote about her relationship with God, family love, friendship, and her love of nature. She viewed nature as an expression of God's love for man. The whole universe was created for man, and man through bringing sin into the world caused God to curse the universe.

Some religions have a distorted concept of nature being God. God created nature and we can see his hand in it, but nature is not God. Heaven in Sweet Adeline's concept involve a divine combination of physicality and spirituality. She saw the beauty in nature as God's gift to man. She frequently wrote about that beauty. She especially was drawn to trees and birds but enjoyed all aspects of beauty in nature.

Following is a sampling of her poetic reflections on nature. In "A Windy Hill" she combines her love for oak trees, birds, and family all in a snapshot that she wants to remember. In "Beautiful Autumn" she combines her love of children at play among autumn leaves. She invites adults to relive that childhood happiness and toss a few leaves in the air, as children do. In the "Last Little Robin" she writes about a robin on a cold fall day.

Mom fed the wild birds and enjoyed their songs. Her childhood was in an area of Missouri that was the northern most boundary of the robin's overwinter range. So, unknowingly to her it would not be unusual to see a robin deep into a mild winter, but her empathy for the well being of the robin would be consistent with her character.

A Windy Hill

As I stood upon a high and windy hill
I gazed below at the plush green earth.
Nestled in the grass stood an old country mill.
It seemed as if time were standing still.

Just beyond was a brilliant golden sunset.
It reflected down on my windows of home.
It looked as if home was a castle of gold
With many great stories yet to be told.

In the distance was a silhouette of an old oak tree
Where it projected an air of mystical wisdom,
Where shadows of little birds were flying to and fro.
They flew for safety to the old oak, they would go.

Magnificent was the beauty I looked upon.
I will always remember that moment of time.
As I turned to my home with windows like gold,
I knew there were more love and beauty to behold.

Beautiful Autumn

As I took a walk on a bright autumn day
I looked upon children at play.
I thought how great to be a child again,
To know not this old world with all its sins.

As they tossed the colorful leaves into the air
They gently drifted to earth here and there.
Their laughter was music to my ears.
They had not a worry or a single fear.

As adults if we would remember these days,
When we used to toss colorful leaves at play
Those old memories will become new.
Just take a walk in the leaves and toss a few!

Last Little Robin

I saw a little robin in the rain.
It was such a cold and dreary day.
Why are you here little robin?
Don't you know its too late for your stay?

The snowflakes will soon be falling.
There will be no fat worms for you to find.
All your feathered friends will miss you so.
Dear little robin are you lost in time?

My little friend, here is some grain for you today.
I will look for you to come back to stay.
As soon as spring is here again.
Today, my friend, you must fly away.

The little robin hopped so very close to me.
He spread his little wings to fly.
As he looked to me, without any fear,
I knew in my heart he was saying goodbye.

Once again Sweet Humble Adeline goes to her Lord with a question that many of us have asked. We have asked this question several times on our discipleship journey. Many times the question comes after a time we drift from the path and want to come back. We yearn to see the beauty we have ignored and then realize and ask, "Am I really worth all the beauty You give me to see?" The answer is the very core of Christianity.

My Garden of Prayer

As I enter my garden of prayer
I know my dear Lord and Savior is there.
The golden sun drifting gently through the trees.
Above me patches of sky as blue as the sea.

The snow-white dove soaring above the land,
The falling autumn leaves painted by God's own
    hand.
It is so peaceful and calm in my garden of prayer
I know my dear Lord and Savior is there.

The beautiful roses all sparkle with dew.
Once again, all the gifts of God become new.
A bird paused in flight and spread its little wings
And perched upon a tiny limb just to sing.

I thank my dear Lord as I dropped to my knees.
Am I really worth all the beauty You give to me?
It was as if I heard a soft gentle voice say to me,
"Yes, my dear child. All I ask is for you to love me."

Mom's biological clock was winding down. She was sleeping quite a bit and she was nearly impossible to arouse. One day my wife and I attended a reception for a relative who had an across-the-country wedding a few weeks before. It was an afternoon affair. My wife and I felt somewhat guilty enjoying the visiting and the delicious food while Adeline was in such a declining state. We shortened our stay at the reception and went to be with Sweet Adeline. My wife settled herself close to Adeline so she could hold her hand and talk softly to her. Mom slept fitfully, often crying out to her "mama." We sat with her but after a time she did not arouse. The staff, more aware than we, knew that her time was near.

We were about to leave and try another day. A favorite nurse's aide quietly entered the room. Without hesitation she approached, turned down the sheet over my mother, got in bed with her, and started rubbing my mother's arms while holding her tenderly and whispering words of comfort directly in my mother's ear. This continued for several minutes. As Mom felt her angelic touch she seemed to relax and breathe easier. It was an honor to witness this caregiver's interaction with my mother. This aide was a friend to Adeline. They joked, teased each other, sang, and danced together. I think they "aided" each other in many ways.

Mom began to arouse. She had a few moments of lucidity and her smile said what needed to be communicated. We had a few words and she faded back to her unconscious state. The angelic aide slipped out of the room not desiring praise; her gift was amazing, appreciated, and given unabashedly.

Upon seeing Adeline resting comfortably we left for home. We felt the need to return the next day before church. There was no need; Mom passed later that night in her sleep. We were concerned that Mom was alone in her last hours, but we were assured by the attending nurse that a steady stream of nurses and aides came to be with her in her sleepful passing.

We come into this world alone and leave this world alone. Or do we? A few days preceding her death she cried out during her semi-unconscious state for the only woman she called "mama." She receded back into her decaying memory banks and called out for Mattie Skillman, her early functional mother. A few days before that, she similarly cried out for Annabel, her "mother" in her formative years. That last night she was lucid for a brief time with her daughter-in-law who became a part of her end time daily routine. I am appreciative that these three women provided a mental glidepath to her physical-spiritual transition. The scriptures tell us that as we pass we will be accompanied by angels to Paradise if we are a believer.

In Jesus' own words in Luke 16:22 [KJV], *"So it was that the beggar died, and was carried by the angels to Abraham's bosom (Paradise)."* Scriptures are ambiguous about the transition for the non-believer.

My mother had that expectation of being accompanied by angels. We will only know for sure when we make that transition ourselves, but my mind has settled on a woman passing through the curtain without fear and possessing excitement to what eternity will bring. After all, she had been preparing for this all her adult life.

What lesson is my Father teaching me? What was the will of the Father in allowing my mother have Satan's Alzheimer's at the end of a well-lived life?

When people were with Sweet Adeline they felt like she was focused and connecting with them. She was a master at raising self-esteem. She affected people's lives—and always for the good. Satan and Alzheimer's did not destroy this inner God-given gift. Three weeks before her death when she was down to sixty-six pounds and had difficulty in walking, she encouraged my wife to walk with her to the cafeteria. After a struggle getting there she saw a new nursing home resident sitting at a table by herself and crying. Even though it caused her to walk further, she hobbled over there and patted the head of the new resident and said some soothing words to her. Typical Adeline.

When we stand back in retrospect and connect the dots of her life, we see that she walked the straight and narrow path and witnessed in the tradition of the Good Samaritan. She raised her children by living the morality that she expressed.

This book has been a tale of a simple woman living a life where God puts you. Alzheimer's and Satan did not defeat her. God and Sweet Adeline won. Her life had a huge positive effect on the lives she touched. My faith tells me that, indeed, she is now in a "better place."

Acknowledgments

My mother lived a singular life that utilized all the Grace given by God to combat all the sorrows multiplied by Satan. Thank you, Sweet Adeline, for your testimony of how, despite stinging setbacks, one can enjoy a fulfilling, meaningful life of love, family, and purpose if you submit to how and where God uses you.

Sweet Adeline's days in the Alzheimer's unit was greatly softened by an angel sent by God that was outside of the bloodline of her family. My wife, Mary, was that angel. She sacrificed hours upon hours of her time by visiting her nearly everyday in the facility. Sometimes it was for just a few minutes and sometimes for hours, but little time elapsed between those sacrificial visits. These types of sacrifices of one's precious life too often get little recognition. How do you recognize a caregiver that does not ask for recognition or payment in delivery of high sacrifice? You pray that they equally have someone to step forward for them. You petition your God for such Grace and hope He hears your prayers.

Thanks to my sister that reviewed, reminded, and recalled Mom's anecdotes; thank you for your support. Linda was a consistent receiver of Mom's examples for she had the most presence through all phases of Sweet

Adeline's empty nest years. They had a special bond that male siblings don't get to enjoy, and Linda is abundantly thankful for Sweet Adeline in her life.

A posthumous thank you goes to Dad that daily, without fail, supported his wife's sacrifices, and contributed his own sacrifices in their 62 years of marriage.

My circle of friends includes many articulate and well-educated people. I take advantage of them by drafting them to read my drafts! Thank you for your proofreading and thank you more for your many years of friendship Carl, Darlene, and Boo.

Katie, Jenny, Adley, Ella, Jackson, Emmy, Jep, Wes, and Nick thank you all for showing interest in your Papa's book. May the book mean more to you in your later years. I love you all.

Robert L. Brunker

About the Author

Robert L. Brunker is the first child of Gilbert and Adeline Brunker. He witnessed sixty-one years of Sweet Adeline's life. As her life lessons took root in his life and he became aware of her "Kitchen Poetry," he started collecting her verses. For over thirty years he wrote what he called retrospections—reflections on how his mother's life examples influenced him and how that was summarized in her various poems. This effort evolved into one of his bucket list items to be completed in his retirement years.

During most of the forty-two years he practiced dentistry, he helped raise two daughters, edited his state's dental journal, went on thirteen medical missions to Jamaica, and engaged his grandchildren in illustrating his first Christian juvenile novel.

He serves on the Board of Elders of his church and continues to make mountains of sawdust from his woodworking projects at the aggravation of his wife of fifty-five years.

Printed in the United States
by Baker & Taylor Publisher Services